A Priest Looks at
Medjugorje

A Priest Looks at
Medjugorje

Rev. Msgr. Richard L. Carroll

VANTAGE PRESS
New York / Los Angeles / Chicago

FIRST EDITION

Copyright © 1989 by Rev. Msgr. Richard L. Carroll

Published by Vantage Press, Inc.
516 West 34th Street, New York, New York 10001

Manufactured in the United States of America
ISBN: 0-533-08358-3

Library of Congress Catalog Card No.: 88-90493

CONTENTS

INTRODUCTION

This small work does not pretend to prove that the apparitions of the Virgin at Medjugorje are true. The Catholic church will adequately address that issue in time.

I have written this book as a witness. I believe Our Blessed Mother has a great love for priests. Mary has seen many of us stumble under the burden of "perfectionism."

Only a mother can lift up a child, brush away its tears, and heal its self-doubts by a single hug. Mary cured my need to make myself perfect at Medjugorje. Our Lady wants to give that gift to priests considered by the world to be fools, yet known by her as—sons.

This book was also written for each of you who is fortunate enough to see yourself as I did, a sinner. The late Bishop Sheen wrote: "I thank God I am a sinner. Now I can have Jesus Christ as my Savior."

Our Blessed Mother is once again doing what she does best—bringing us to Jesus Christ. Her message is a clarion warning: Tremendous trials await the world. Peace is a gift from Jesus Christ. Prayer and penance are the fuel of love.

Surrender to the Cross of Jesus Christ. You, too, can have Peace of Soul. This is a promise from a woman who calls herself "Queen of Peace."

A Priest Looks at
Medjugorje

Chapter 1

MESSAGE OF MEDJUGORJE

Numerous claims have been made about apparitions of our Blessed Mother. There are at least two hundred reported visions of Mary since 1930 that the Catholic Church has not recognized.

The Church is very cautious in approving phenomena. Lourdes and Fatima are two of the most famous shrines in existence in which the apparitions have been sanctioned as worthy of belief.

Medjurgorje is in the Catholic Croatian region of Hercegovina. The village in Yugoslavia is called Bijakovici. The parish is St. James, Medjugorje.

On June 24, 1981, the feast of John the Baptist, two girls, Ivanka Ivankovic and Mirjana Dragicevic, were taking a walk on the nearby mountain. They spotted a luminous silhouette. It was the form of a young girl in a gray robe whose face was shining gently. They realized it was the Virgin Mary. They returned to town and picked up four friends to go back with them: Vicka Ivankovic, Ivan Ivankovic, Ivan Dragicevic and Milka Pavlovic. When they returned, all six of the children saw the apparition.

The next day, June 25, they returned at the same time, 6:15 P.M. Two new young people came for the first time, Marija Pavlovic and Jakov Colo. Milka Pavlovic did not return, since she had to work, nor did Ivan Ivankovic, who thought the adventure too childish.

1

Once again these children saw the Virgin and were filled with happiness. The six who were present on June 25 have continued to receive the apparitions. Marjana Dragicevic has stopped seeing the visions after December 25. Since then, the group has numbered five.

On the second day of the apparitions, two older people were brought along, but they saw nothing.

On June 26, Milka returned with the others but did not see the vision, nor has she seen it since.

The children recited the rosary, as well as the prayers traditional to their area—namely the Our Father seven times, Hail Marys, and Glory Be to the Father. The Virgin told them to add the Creed. Vicka, the most outgoing, sprinkled the vision with holy water, telling her, "If you are not the Virgin, please leave." The Virgin smiled.

On June 27, the six children were brought by the police to Citluk to be interrogated. They were also given a psychiatric examination by Dr. Antr Vujevic. The psychiatrist determined the children were completely normal.

On Sunday, June 28, fifteen thousand people gathered on the mountain in expectation. This was clearly something that the communist authorities would have to watch closely.

On Monday, June 29, the children were once again interrogated at Citluk. Another psychiatrist, Dr. Dzuda, examined the children and found them to be healthy.

On June 30 two women came to take the children on a trip, hoping to get their minds off this phenomenon. Five of the six went, all except Ivan.

At Bijakovici, when they were returning, the children asked that they stop the car. They were at Cerno near Ljubuski, which is in sight of their hill. There the children knelt and once again they were able to see the Virgin. It was on this occasion that they asked Mary to begin visiting them in the church since the police had forbidden them to go to the original site. The Virgin agreed.

They gathered in the church daily. They began by saying the rosary with the crowd that was present. At 6:00 P.M. the children would leave the church and go to a small room, fourteen feet by fifteen feet, which is opposite the sacristy. The apparitions took place in this room. At a later day the children were moved from the sacristy to the rectory for the apparitions. At present, they are in the choir loft.

Once inside the small room they began praying, standing, saying seven times the Our Father, Hail Mary, and Glory Be, as well as the Creed. When the children see the Virgin, in unison they fall to their knees. The few who are fortunate enough to be present watch as the visionaries are wrapped in ecstacy. The children recite the second part of the Our Father, Mary saying the first part as well as the Creed.

After the vision ends, they return to the main body of the church for mass. The children disperse, some acting as servers or singing in the choir. At the end of mass, a hymn is sung and the traditional prayer of the region recited. It is not unusual to have as many as 10,000 visitors present in and outside of the church.

One of the most interesting insights given by the children is a description of Mary. The children agree that she has black curly hair, blue eyes, rosy cheeks, and is slender and beautiful.

She is covered with a veil flowing over a robe that is impossible to describe. The gown seems to be a coffee and cream color. She is so beautiful, one child remarked, that you just want to look at her.

The parish of Medjugorje is dominated by a cross that was erected on Sipovac Hill in 1933. This cross (*kriz*) resulted in the name of the mountain being changed to Krizevac.

On August 21, 1984, one hundred and fifty people were on the hill praying when they experienced a phenomenon of light. The sun was seen by them as a great heart. Underneath were six small hearts. The people were filled with fear and began to weep and pray.

On other occasions, people have seen light in the form of a column that appears on the hill. In October of 1981, a large flame shot up in the air. It lasted ten or fifteen minutes. No cause could be found to explain this.

Those who have the opportunity to meet the children—whose ages vary from the oldest, born in 1964, to the youngest, born in 1971—are deeply impressed. There is a tremendous sense of friendship. They do not argue with one another, nor are they jealous. They are polite and dress just like their peers. The major change that has taken place in them is a deepening of their faith in Christ and His Church.

The children were asked to inquire from the Virgin what title she wished to use. She told them, "I am the Queen of Peace." It seems obvious from this that her message to the world involves peace. Her message to priests through the children was to safeguard the Faith.

These apparitions have clearly put the Francisan priests at odds with the Marxist government. The pastor, Father Jozo Zovko, was arrested and charged with crimes against the state. In a sermon discussing the forty years Moses was in the desert, the communist listener thought he was talking about the forty years of Marxist rule. The communist leaders were apprehensive, since it was here that Tito had killed 2500 people. Father Zovko was sentenced to three and a half years in jail; it was commuted to one and a half years. Father Zrinko Cuvalo, another Franciscan, became pastor. Father Tomislaw Vlasic was named assistant.

The people of this area have been greatly changed by these visions. There is a new sense of the need to do penance. It is now customary that many of the people of the community, in addition to the children, fast two days a week—Wednesday and Friday. Two of the children fast on Saturday as well. The fast consists of eating bread and water three times a day. They may also eat fruit.

The children explained that fasting brings a sense of joy, a total abandonment to God. As one of the children said, "I think we are the happiest people on the earth."

It was significant that Mary reminded Catholics of the importance of Confession. There have been occasions when as many as seventy priests have heard confessions of the multitude of pilgrims.

The Virgin insisted on the urgency in believing her message: "Many people will not believe you and many fervent believers will grow cold, but as for you, remain firm and exhort people to urgent prayer," she said.

In the first apparition Mary said nothing. On June 25, 1981, Mirjana asked her for a sign, since people would say they were taking drugs. Mary did not answer but began praying the local traditional prayers already mentioned. They sang the Maranatha together with her, "Come, Lord, come" (1 Cor. 16:22). The following day she told them she was the Blessed Virgin Mary.

On June 27 she told them, "Peace, peace, nothing but peace. Men must be reconciled with God and with one another. For this to happen, it is necessary to believe, to pray, to fast, to go to Confession."

In the following days Mary recommended that traditional prayer be added to the Creed. The Creed reiterates our belief in God the Father, Son, and Holy Spirit; the fact that Jesus Christ was born of the Virgin Mary, suffered and died, and rose from the dead. It is also an affirmation of the Church.

On August 6, 1981, the message of peace was written in the sky, *Mir* (peace). This was repeated several times and witnessed by many. At the end of August 1981, Mary said, "I am the Queen of Peace."

On September 4 Mary promised that a permanent sign would appear after all of the children have received ten messages in their entirety. This sign will be for all unbelievers.

At present some of the children have received all of the messages; some have not.

Mary told the children something interesting about Russia: "Russia is the place where God will be most glorified." On December 8, 1981, the children saw the Virgin beseeching Christ, "My beloved Son, I beg You to pardon the world for the heavy sins by which it offends You." Seven months later they were told that "prayer and fasting can prevent even war."

On August 6, 1981, the Blessed Mother recommended monthly confession. This practice was begun in the parish. At the beginning of each month there is a triduum, including the liturgy, which is preceded by an adoration of the blessed sacrament on Thursday. Confessors are kept busy all day.

In the spring of 1983, Mary implored, "Hasten your conversation. You who believe, be converted and deepen your faith." On April 20 in tears, the Virgin said, "I want to convert them, but they are not converted. Pray! Pray for them. Do not wait."

June 16, 1983, her message was as follows: "I have come to tell the world that God is truth. He exists. In Him is true happiness and abundance of life. I present myself here as Queen of Peace. Oh, tell the world that peace is necessary for the salvation of the world. In God is found true joy from which flows true peace."

On June 28 she said, "You pray too little. Pray at least half an hour morning and evening. Consecrate five minutes to the Sacred Heart. Every family is its image."

In July the Virgin said, "Be alert. This is a dangerous time for you. The devil will try to turn you from this way. Those who give themselves to God will be the object of attack."

On August 2, 1983: "Consecrate yourselves to the Immaculate Heart. Abandon yourself totally. I will protect you. I will pray to the Holy Spirit. Pray to Him yourselves." She added later, "The trouble comes from Satan."

In October, Mary had this message for the entire community: "All the families should consecrate themselves to the Sacred Heart of Jesus every day. I would be very happy if the whole family were to come together for prayer every morning for a half hour."

Because the ten secrets are to be revealed to the world when all of the children have received them and because it was said that the secrets implied punishments and catastrophes, Mary was asked about the dramatic future. She replied, "This comes from false prophets. They say 'on such a day at such a time will be a catastrophe.' I have always said the evil (the punishment) will come if the world is not converted. Call people to conversion. Everything depends on your conversion."

Although the apparitions continue, they are definitely coming to an end. In the beginning they lasted for twenty minutes. Now they last a very short time. Mirjana and Ivanka have already received the ten secrets. As soon as all have received them, Mary will allow them to make them known. She will then leave a permanent sign on the hill on which the first apparitions took place.

At this time there are up to thirty or forty thousand visitors a day to this tiny place. What are the key elements of this message to the world?

The message is urgent. The world is now in a state of self-destruction, without order or meaning, and sin abounds. The threat is due to the fact that countless people have given themselves over to sin. Prayer and penance can change all of this.

God exists, and He loves us. The communists deny His existence. The materialists in the West act as if He doesn't exist.

Reconciliation is a need. We must repent and be converted. At Medjugorje, when Mary talks of sin, it is in order to bring us to conversion, knowing that all happiness comes from God.

It is clear at Medjugorje that there is a thirst for prayer.

People are making time for God. Even the young people have been asked to spend a half hour at prayer in the morning and a half hour in the evening.

Another aspect of the message of Medjugorje is to reaffirm the Gospel call to fasting—fasting not by law or rule, as many older Catholics remember, but as was done in the early Church, always linked to prayer.

Fasting has almost disappeared in the Church today. It was seen as a law, not a means of life, an opening to prayer. It is not a radical fast. People adjust the fast to their health. We should remember that our primary fast is from sin. We can also fast from the hours spent viewing television. Fasting is meant to add intensity to our prayer life. The people fasting eat moderately three times a day—bread, water, and fruit, if necessary. It sounds reminiscent of John the Baptist's message—repentance, prayer, and fasting.

The most vital question, of course, is this: "Are these apparitions real?" The arguments speak loudly for the authenticity of these apparitions, although they do not yet have the official sanction of the Church. Approval is never given quickly, although the preponderance of signs seems to indicate their believability.

There are no doctrinal problems with these apparitions. There is no exclusive concentration on Mary. Through the daily celebration of mass, the people are brought to Christ. Father Tomislav Vlasic asked Vicka, one of the children, "Do you experience the Virgin as the one who gives graces or as one who prays to God?" She answered, "As someone who prays to God."

The Virgin encourages openness and ecumenism. She told the children, "We must respect every man in his faith. It is never right to look down on a man because of his convictions. The believers are separated one from another, but God directs all the Christian groups as a king directs his subjects by means of his ministers. Jesus Christ is the sole mediator of salvation. The power of the Holy Spirit is not equally strong in all the churches."

When asked about their future vocations, Mary is not a possessive mother. She told them, "I would like you to become priests and nuns, but only if you desire it. You are free. It is for you to choose."

Our Lady leads us to Christ. When asked what prayer was best, she said, "It is the mass and you will never be able to exhaust its greatness. That is why you should be there humbly and prepared." The rosary and the preparation flow into the mass. Mary has appeared showing Christ to the children in His childhood and in His passion.

Another positive sign of authenticity is the children themselves. They are completely normal individuals. Each has his or her own personality. These visions have deepened their prayer life and their faith.

Finally, the community itself has been lead to a deep experience of prayer and penance. They are an inspiration to the visitors. A professor from Dusseldorf said of them, "I have traveled the whole world, and I have never seen people like these. They are alive." Another visitor said, "I did not see the face of the Virgin, but I saw her reflection in the face of the people there." The late David Duplessis, a non-Catholic Pentecostal leader, said, "Despite all my contacts with the Catholic Church, I have been afraid of your Catholic tradition concerning Mary because she does not occupy such a place among us. Among you I have come to understand that Mary leads to Christ."

Perhaps the most significant aspect of Medjugorje is a new call that we had forgotten—to prayer and conversion, to penance and fasting. It is an awakening of a living faith.

In November 1983, Marija Pavlovic requested that the pastor send a report concerning the urgency of the message of

Medjugorje to the pope, which he did.

Father Vlasic complied with her request on December 2, 1983. The report to Pope John Paul II stressed the following:

1. There are five young people who see an apparition of the Blessed Virgin Mary daily.
2. Mary repeatedly calls us to reconciliation and conversion. She promised a visible sign at the site of the apparitions of Medjugorje.
3. Mary promised to disclose ten secrets to us. These apparitions are the last that Our Lady will give; hence, they are lasting for a long period of time.
4. Before the visible sign, there will be three warnings. These warnings will be in the form of events on the earth.
5. The sign will be given to prove that the apparitions are true and to bring people back to the faith.
6. The ninth and tenth secrets are serious. They contain chastisement for the sins of the world. Punishment is inevitable. Prayer and penance will lessen the severity.
7. There is time for conversion . . . but the time is short.
8. The events predicted by Mary are near; hurry to be converted.
9. Mirjana added a warning Mary gave her. This is the century of Satan. His power will be destroyed. He is responsible for destroying marriages and creating divisions among priests and is responsible for obsessions and murder. You must protect yourselves through prayer and fasting, especially community prayer. Carry blessed objects with you, put them in your home and restore the use of holy water.

According to some experts Pope Leo XIII had an apocalyptic vision of the Church. He introduced the prayer to St. Michael which was said after masses up to the time of the second Vatican council. The children were shown the contents of the letter sent to the pope and their bishop. They agreed that the contents were true. For a complete history of these apparitions, read *Is the Virgin Mary Appearing at Medjugorje?*, by Rene Laurentin, Word Among Us Press, P.O. Box 369, Gaithersburg, MD 20877-0369.

Chapter II

A TRIP TO MEDJUGORJE

After nearly twenty-eight years as a priest, I was "burnt out." The archbishop granted me an eight months' sabbatical beginning December 3, 1986. My illness might better be labeled "perfectionism."

From the time I was a thirteen-year-old student in the minor seminary I was expected to be as "perfect as your Heavenly Father is Perfect." Celibacy, the renunciation of the right to marry, I was told, would result in becoming a saint. Sadly I learned that this inordinant desire to make myself holy, "perfectionism," was an impossibility. Even my seventy-hour work weeks would not bring me closer to my cherished goal of intimacy with God.

The result was bitter anger! I was filled with fury at the Church for misleading me. I was resentful at her for doing nothing to lighten the burden that resulted in more than one hundred thousand priests worldwide abandoning the ministry, primarily because of celibacy and disillusionment. I was angry with the Church for placing priests in the middle of the contraception issue that caused 25 percent of American Catholics to desert the Church. Priests were blamed for being either too liberal or too conservative. Yet in my heart I knew it was less important that we be perceived as right than that we be seen as caring.

I was angry with myself for not leaving the priesthood years earlier. My perfectionism had resulted in deep loneliness.

Yet somehow I could not leave my children, my parishioners, as orphans.

Not even God was spared my wrath. He had sent me one burden after another. Suicides, teen pregnancies, alcoholism, and infant deaths were all testimony to a God who didn't care. Yet I was expected to champion His cause and explain his unfeeling actions to His children.

When the pain became unbearable, the loneliness extreme, I came to realize that the price for perfectionism was too high. I was "burnt out." I received permission to be absent from my parish to begin my sabbatical.

My sabbatical would not have been complete without a visit to Medjugorje. Somehow I knew that it had to be on March 25, the feast of the Annunciation. The tour company I contacted offered me the opportunity of serving as chaplain on March 7, 1987. Never one to turn down a free trip, I agreed. However, I stumbled on an open drawer during the middle of the night and broke one of my toes. Therefore, I had to delay the trip. I arrived in Medjugorje on March 25, at midnight.

It had been a long trip—a flight from New Orleans to Pittsburgh, then New York City. The Yugoslavian airliner was delayed three hours. We arrived in Belgrade after a long flight. Next were two short domestic flights, first to Zagreb, then to Dubrovnik. It was 9:00 P.M. before we boarded a bus, which would wend its way through the mountains for three hours on the last leg of our journey to Medjugorje.

There were forty-one pilgrims in our group. We were divided into four different homes. There were eleven in our house, four downstairs and seven upstairs.

The program in Medjugorje would remain the same from Wednesday until Sunday. We would gather for breakfast at 8:00 A.M. The English mass was celebrated at 10:00 A.M. Lunch would be at 1:00 P.M. There would be a concelebrated mass in Croatian at 6:00 P.M. Dinner would be served after 8:00 P.M.

The first highlight took place in the Room of Apparitions Wednesday afternoon, the feast of the Annunciation. I had arrived outside the room at 3:00 P.M. to be certain I would gain access. At four I was ushered into the rectory. At 5:00 P.M. a Franciscan priest led a small group inside the room.

This was one of the most moving moments of my life. The visionaries present this day, Marija and Jakov, knelt to say the rosary. They took turns leading it. Those inside the room answered.

There were huge tears running down my cheeks. What was the miracle that I sought that day? It was healing. My tears were not just for me, but for the countless priests who, like me, hurt so badly. I needed to know that Mary still loved us—that she still loves me despite my sinfulness and my anger.

I wanted to be that eight-year-old child I remembered who loved Mary so much. I needed a return to innocence. As we prayed the rosary, the love for Mary that I seemed to have lost over the years reappeared. Once again she was not just the Mother of Jesus; she was also my mother. I was filled with love. This was the gift of the Holy Spirit, given through her intercession.

The forty-five minutes passed quickly. After reciting the rosary kneeling, the children began to move their lips in unison. Those in the room with the visionaries could not hear a sound. We were all anxious to learn the message Mary had given that particular day. The message read to us the next day went like this:

Dear Children:
    Today I thank you for your presence in this place where I give special graces. I call upon each one of you to start living the life God wants from you and to start

doing good deeds of love and generosity. I don't want you, dear children, to live the messages and commit the sins which I do not like. Therefore, dear children, I want each of you to live the new life without destroying everything God creates in you and gives you. I give you my special blessing, and I remain with you on your way to conversion. Thank you for your response to my call.

It seemed to me that the message, as important as it is, was not nearly as significant as what Mary had done for me that day. In a moment she had cured my self-hatred. She had made me realize that she loved me and every priest very much. She knows the trials we have faced. She still loves us.

On Thursday a small group went up to the Hill of Apparitions. Mary first appeared to the children on this hillside. Only later, after the authorities objected, the visions continued first in the church sacristy and then in the rectory.

The following day many of our group went up Mount Krizevac. This was quite a climb. Many years ago the people had erected a cross on the top of the mountain. There are stations of the cross going up the mountain. It took two and a half hours to climb the mountain and pray the stations.

The prayerful mood of the group in our house was broken by a funny experience. A young woman about twenty-five had washed her clothes and put them on a heater to dry. The clothes caught on fire. One of the men in her house threw the clothes on the floor in the bathroom. She began stomping on them, trying to put the fire out. The bottoms of her pajamas caught fire and began racing up her legs. One of the men, seeing the flames, began tugging on her pants to pull them off. In her modesty she tried to keep them on, despite the fact that she was on fire. Finally, danger overcame modesty, and she slipped out of her burning garment and escaped injury.

Friday, March 27, was a very special day at Medjugorje.

I had returned from Mount Krizevac about 4:00 P.M. and decided to rest before the 6:00 P.M. mass. After fifteen minutes, I realized that the Lord wanted me to do more praying. So I got up and began walking toward the church. Our house was about a mile from the church.

As I walked along, I experienced what many others have seen: the miracle of the sun. The best way I can explain it, it seemed that the sun appeared like the host in the Monstrance. There were colors emanating from the host.

I thanked the Lord for this little sign of grace. I was determined not to look too long, as some people injure their eyes looking at the sun. My heart was full of praise and joy as I walked along to church. This experience is common to many who visit Medjugorje.

By now our group had become very childlike. One of the ladies called it "Mary's summer camp."

Another phenomenon occurred to some people on our tour. I doubt if I would have believed it had I not seen it myself. Four of our group had their rosaries changed—the silver turned to gold; another woman, whose daughter did not want her mother to go on the pilgrimage, had a silver locket belonging to the daughter. This locket turned to polished gold. The inside of the locket remained silver. We learned that two young attorneys saw the cross on the mountain surrounded by light. When they investigated this, they could find no reason for the illumination.

As exciting as these little signs were, I was most impressed with the visionaries. We met Ivanka first. She has received the ten messages and no longer goes in the Room of Apparitions. She has married and is helping her young husband run a coffee shop near the church. She was obviously shy and retiring, but peace seemed to permeate her being.

We met Vicka a few days after she had returned from the hospital. She is suffering from a tumor of the brain. Her mother asked her why she didn't request Mary to cure her. She replied that many are brought back to Jesus through her suffering.

But Marija was the greatest blessing our Lady shared with me. Through Helga, an interpreter, we met with her twice. We learned from Marija that Mary seemed very real, very loving to her. "She hugged us as our own mothers did," she said. She stressed the need for prayer and penance. It was obvious that fasting on bread and water was very important.

Mary warned the children of the power of the devil. His power extends even to this place of Mary's apparitions. Marija said that they were told that there were many people in hell. They learned that many go to purgatory before reaching heaven. Some of the children had visions of hell and purgatory.

I asked Marija if Mary was upset that one of the visionaries had married. She replied that Mary had blessed Ivanka before her marriage. It is a sacrament, she reminded me.

I wanted to know how they were able to keep their secrets. "Isn't it true women cannot keep secrets?" I asked. "Perhaps it is my masculine nature," she replied. "No, no, no!" we all shouted.

"Did Mary speak of the end of the world?" I asked.

"She did not," she replied.

On our second visit on Sunday, I gave Marija a present. I had bought a black windreaker for the trip. I presented it to her, together with my cap and scarf.

Saturday, March 28, was my second opportunity to be present in the Room of Apparitions. I was the last person allowed in the room. Marija was the only visionary present on that day. She entered the room and knelt down next to me, less than two feet away. I was filled with awe. It was if Our Blessed Mother herself was saying that she would remain close to me.

Even the power of Satan is visible in this place. The owner of our travel agency had an inkling. When she was taking a shower in the home where she was staying, the tile began to fly off the wall. It didn't just fall off; it literally flew off the wall. She had to use her towel to escape being cut when she got out of the tub.

Another great blessing occurred on Saturday morning. Our group was allowed to celebrate mass in the small chapel on the right side of the church. This was the room where Our Blessed Mother appeared to the children for a period of time.

The members of our group huddled in this small area. There was a great sense of love and peace during this mass.

The same day I decided that I would buy rosaries for many of the schoolchildren. I asked the Franciscan in charge of the religious-articles store if he took Visa. He answered he did. After counting out 850 rosaries, the bill came to $1050. I handed him my Visa card. He thought I had travelers checks. The Visa card was not acceptable. I attempted to get travelers' checks at the bank, to no avail. Three young women on our tour loaned me all of the money.

Unfortunately, when we returned, my suitcase with all of the rosaries was stolen in the airport in New York on March 31. I received a letter from security a few days later, telling me that they could not locate the bag. I received a call from Father Gallagher, my associate pastor, on Holy Saturday, April 18. The suitcase containing the rosaries was returned to Slidell without explanation. Not even Satan will mess with that Lady.

At the end of May our group had a reunion. A young woman was finally able to tell me that she had seen Mary one night at Medjugorje. After fifteen minutes of watching the vision, she left to come get me, only to see the vision disappear. It took her months before she could even talk about it.

Doubtless many of you have heard of other phenomena. The day I returned to Slidell, a woman stopped in the office to show me a rosary that not only changed to gold but now had the picture of the Sacred Heart on the back of the medal that connects the beads. She has had the rosary for thirteen years. Another parishioner gave me a picture of a bush taken at Medjugorje. Unexplainably the image of Mary is in the picture holding a rosary. These small gifts can cause us to lose sight of the central message of Mary—prayer and penance. I believe these little signs are given to help us become more childlike. For Jesus himself said, "Unless you become like little children, you will not enter the kingdom of heaven."

Medjugorje was one of the greatest blessings of my life. I realized that peace truly is a gift of the Holy Spirit. I now know that Mary loves me, that she loves all priests, she loves you, her children. I have committed myself to teach our children her message of prayer and penance. I am convinced that we will undergo great trials in the coming years; but because of the great love for Jesus Christ present in the Blessed Sacrament, our community will not only survive but will prosper. Satan is real—make no mistake about this. But Mary is far more powerful. My sabbatical was her gift, not only to me but to each of you, to help us during the trials predicted to the children that are soon to occur. In the end there will be a period of great peace. It was promised by a warm loving mother who chose to call herself the Queen of Peace.

Chapter III

PRAYER

I am sure many of you wonder how I spent my eight months on sabbatical. I shared with you one special week at Medjurgorje. The rest of the time, in addition to prayer, study and reading, was spent writing a book. It all began this way. As I was preparing to go on the sabbatical, I met with a priest friend who is a psychologist. He had encourged me to take the time off to regain my good health. He discouraged me from joining any structured program. "What would you like to do most of all?" he asked. I told Father Bill about a book I had just read. The author asked the question, "What would you do if you had only six months left to live?" "I would write a book," I told Bill. "Then do it," he said. "Of course, it won't be published." "Why not?" he asked. "Do it." I now realize that the book I wrote was for my own benefit.

As I reread the book I realized that many of the ideas on Medjugorje should be separated from the original. These are contained in this labor of love titled *A Priest Looks at Medjugorje*.

I would like to share with you some thoughts on prayer. The two key elements of Our Lady's message were on prayer and penance. We will consider the message of our Blessed Mother on the subject of prayer, which she taught the children.

We can learn an interesting lesson from Elijah. It is an important one. The Lord was not in the wind; He was not in the earthquake, nor was He in the fire. He was in the tiny whispering sound. We will not find him in the winds of addic-

20

tions. We will not find him in the rubble of accumulated wealth and power. We will not find him in the fire of passion or perversion. But we will find him in the tiny whispering sound of prayer.

One of the most important truths Mary taught us was the need for prayer. We do not pray enough. In May 1983, our Blessed Mother asked Jelena Vasilj, then eleven years old, to begin a prayer group in Medjugorje. Mary promised she would lead these children. The group would have a priest guide, Father Vlasic.

How do they pray? They meditate in silence, they pray aloud spontaneously, sometimes they pray the Rosary.

To be a member each must be willing to give him- or herself to Jesus in the following manner:

1. Pray at least three hours a day.
2. Those who work or go to school must pray half an hour in the morning, half an hour in the evening.
3. Commit to daily mass.
4. Fast on bread and water on Wednesdays and Fridays.
5. Consecrate themselves each day to the hearts of Jesus and Mary.
6. After a month's period of prayer and fasting, they must make a four-year commitment.

There are sixty-three youths in the group.

Our Blessed Mother has given the visionaries important information on prayer. I would like to share with you some of Mary's thoughts on this subject:

"Dear children, today also I would like to call you to persistent prayer and penance. Especially let the young people of this parish be more active in their prayer."

"Pray, pray. Prayer will give you everything. It is through prayer that you can obtain everything."

21

"Dear children, today I want to call you; pray, pray, pray. In prayer you will come to know the greatest joy and the way out of every situation that has no way out. Thank you for moving ahead in prayer. Every individual is dear to my heart, and I thank all of you who have rekindled prayer in your families."

MARY AND THE ROSARY: "I ask you, I ask everyone to pray the rosary. You will overcome all the trouble which Satan is trying to inflict on the Church. Let all priests pray the rosary. Give time to the rosary."

OUR LADY RECOMMENDS DEVOTION TO JESUS IN THE BLESSED SACRAMENT and she speaks often of his heart and of his wound: "This evening, dear children, in a special way I am grateful to you for being here. Continually adore the Most Holy Sacrament. I am always present when the faithful are in adoration. Special graces are then being received."

OUR LADY SPEAKS FREQUENTLY OF THE HOLY SPIRIT: "Tomorrow night pray for the Spirit of truth. Especially you from the parish. The Spirit of truth is necessary for you in order to convey the messages just as I give them to you. Pray that the Holy Spirit will renew your parish. If people assist at mass in a half-hearted fashion, they return home with cold, empty hearts."

FAMILY PRAYER: "Today I call you to a renewal of family prayer in your homes. Let prayer take the first place in your families."

PRAYER AND SCRIPTURE: "I ask you to read the Bible in your homes every day and let it be in a visible place there so that it always encourages you to read and pray."

PRAYER AS A WEAPON AGAINST SATAN: "Dear children, these days Satan is trying to thwart all my plans. Pray that his plan may not be fulfilled. I will pray to my son Jesus that he will give you the grace to experience his victory in Satan's temptations.

"Pray that Satan flees from the parish and from every individual who comes to the parish. Prayer is the only way that leads to peace. If you pray and fast, you will obtain all you ask."

Finally, it is important to realize that each of us prays as the Holy Spirit leads us. St. Paul wrote to the Corinthians, "There are varieties of gifts but the same spirit, and there are varieties of service but the same Lord, and there are varieties of working but it is the same God who inspires them all in everyone" (I Cor. 12:4).

This is how each of the five visionaries likes to pray:

Vicka: "I can say even ten rosaries, but I am not made for meditation. God has not given me that gift."

Marija: "I gladly say a rosary, but I prefer to meditate; I simply must retire into solitude; I remain in silence."

Ivan: "The Bible is the biggest thing in my prayer."

Ivanka: "Sometimes I use the Bible but seldom. I talk to Jesus in my own words. Pray with the heart."

Jakov: "Prayer is the most precious thing in my whole life. Every prayer is a conversation with God, heart to heart."*

Regardless what form of prayer you select, remember. Paul's admonition: "No one can say Jesus is Lord except by the Holy Spirit."

Let us close with an act of Consecration given by Mary to one of the children: "O my Mother, Mother of Goodness, of love and mercy, I love you immensely; I offer myself to you through your goodness, love and mercy save me. I wish to be yours. I love you immensely, and I wish you to keep me. I beg you with all my heart, Mother of Goodness, give me your goodness that with it I may reach paradise. I beg you in your immense love to give me the grace to love everybody as you

---

*Rene Laurentin, *Is the Virgin Mary Appearing at Medjugorje?* (Gaithersburg, MD, Word Among Us Press). Used by permission.

loved Jesus Christ. I beg you also for grace that I may be full of mercy and you. I offer myself completely to you, and I wish that you would stay with me at every step because you are full of grace. I wish I may never forget these graces; and if I lose them, I ask you to return them to me. Amen."

Chapter IV

PENANCE

The community of St. Margaret Mary was asked to make a commitment of time and talent to Jesus Christ. I would ask you to consider a ministry to your own children. This will implement the message of Our Blessed Mother at Medjugorje—namely, prayer and penance.

I am an addict, a food addict. At times I could kill for chocolate; chocolate-chip cookies never last in my house.

Many of you are also addicts—food addicts like me. Anyone who eats or drinks in order to change his mood rather than for nourishment is a food addict. The alcoholic drinks excessively for the same reasons; a food addict overeats whenever depressed, bored, or lonely, trying to overcome these hurtful emotions.

I believe that the Lord taught me an important lesson on my sabbatical. I am convinced that the warnings given by our Blessed Mother are real. At least two of the ten secrets given to the children and soon to be revealed involve punishment to mankind unless we do prayer and penance. This, as you know, is a reiteration of her warning at Fatima in 1917, a warning we failed to heed. It seems to me that these punishments may well involve addictions. If the warnings about AIDS come to pass and 100 million die worldwide by the year 2000, we will see that this is caused primarily by addiction to drugs or illicit sex.

Addictive behavior will be the peril during the coming

days. There will be addictions to sex, both natural and unnatural. There will be addictions to food, drugs, and alcohol. Addictions to TV, money, power, and prestige will cause the downfall of many.

I believe that the cure for addiction is the cross of Jesus Christ. You recall in the Book of Numbers, in the Old Testament, people were rebelling in the desert. For punishment, God sent serpents that bit many of the people; these people died. The Jews begged Moses to pray. In answer to his prayer, Moses was told, "Make a serpent and mount it on a pole; and if anyone who had been bitten looks at it, he will recover." Moses made a bronze serpent and mounted it on a pole; and whenever anyone who had been bitten looked at the serpent, he recovered.

Jesus used this image when he told the people that just as the serpent was lifted up in the desert, so too the son of man would be lifted up. He meant, of course, the cross. Those who looked upon the cross of Jesus would be saved. So too, in our day, the cross will be the reminder. It is the cross of Jesus that can cure addictive behavior.

Jesus was once asked by his disciples why they had been unable to cast out demons from a man. Jesus replied, "These demons can be cast out only by prayer and fasting." This is the same message of Medjugorje. The cross is the sign of prayer and penance, the cure for addictive behavior.

The Holy Spirit taught me the need to teach the school children to do penance and to pray. If they are to be prepared to face and conquer addiction in their own lives, they must master basic scriptural concepts and put them into practice by learning to say no in little things.

The cross at Medjugorje is a key sign. Many signs of supernatural intervention have taken place on the mountain near the cross. It is a call to do penance, to fight the power of evil in our lives. It is a sign heard from Calvary—the blood of Jesus can cure you.

I offered a program for the grade-school children beginning in the third grade in the parochial school and CCD starting late in September 1987. It was totally voluntary. Those children who wished to participate signed a contract between themselves and Our Blessed Mother. It reads: "Because of my love for Jesus and a desire to please you, My Mother Mary, by praying and doing penance, I agree to work to be fit for life spiritually and physically, mentally and emotionally, for the next nine months. The program consists of the following:

"1. Prayer: At least fifteen minutes every day, ideally thirty minutes.
"2. Penance:
"A. Give up junk food at least four times a week. Junk food includes potato chips, onion rings, French fries, cookies, candy, coke, milk shakes, donuts, pastry, and all food high in fats, such as Whoppers, Big Macs, and pizzas.
"B. Reduce TV by at least one hour a day for prayer time and exercise, as well as studies. (The average child watches five hours of TV daily.)
"C. Thirty minutes of aerobic exercises, preferable walking or bicycle riding.
"D. One act of kindness each day.
"E. Maintain a spiritual diary containing successes and failures."

It should be obvious that children will never learn penance—saying NO to themselves—without the support of their parents. As important as other ministries are in the Church, none are as imperative as that to your own children. I asked parents of those children who participated to do the following:

1. Be supportive by words and acts of encouragement.
2. Buy and serve foods low in saturated fat and sugar. (Nu-

tritional needs of children include limiting fat to 30% of their total calories, according to the American Heart Association.)

3. Support by giving one hug a day.
4. Review the daily diary weekly.
5. Reward the effort, even when it is not perfect, by a gift of 25 cents a week. This will be your child's gift to a starving child in Africa.
6. Initiate family prayer or accompany the child to adoration if possible.
7. Encourage family exercise activites, such as family walks or bicycling. Activities at church will be offered.
8. Recognize the power of example. If you fail to pray or do penance, if you do not act lovingly, it will hurt your child. If you are above or below your ideal weight, we encourage you to participate in a church-sponsored nutritional program.

Our Blessed Mother is calling us to live out her messages at Medjugore of prayer and penance. If our children are going to overcome the addictions offered by Satan, they must be taught. You will be witness to the power of the love of Jesus Christ to heal addiction. May the Holy Spirit give you the courage to begin.

Chapter V

THE HOLY SPIRIT,
A PLAYFUL GOD

In September 1987 I gave to each of the schoolchildren a rosary blessed by our Mother Mary at Medjugorje. I told at St. Margaret Mary of the struggle involved in borrowing $1,000.00 to purchase the rosaries, only to have my suitcase, with the rosaries, stolen in New York City.

I recounted how our Blessed Mother's special love for them caused the good thief to return these rosaries that had been stolen. I asked each of them to say the rosary every day.

Our Blessed Mother asked us through the children at Medjugorje to pray. I am sure Mary would love to see each of you saying her rosary every night with your family. If you can't convince them to do so, bring your rosary to bed and say it alone every night.

This will become the most important fifteen minutes of your day, as you honor Our Blessed Mother.

I have shared with our community some of the wonderful things I learned at Medjugorje. I discovered that peace was a gift that comes to us from the Holy Spirit himself. I learned that Mary and Jesus love you and me very much.

I was taught that peace will come to all men only when each of us prays daily and does penance. As a consequence of this, I wrote an agreement that I asked each child to make with our Blessed Mother and agree to pray and do penance to bring about her great peace, for she calls herself Queen of Peace.

I would like to share with you the rest of the story. I recount this not in the hope that you might think me better than anyone else.

When I returned from Medjugorje, I felt a great burden to try to encourage the children to fight the power of the devil. I began to realize that Satan traps many through overeating or drinking, excessive television, and later drugs and illicit sex.

When Jesus was asked by his disciples why they could not cast out certain devils, he answered, "These can be thrown out only by prayer and penance."

One night when I was on my sabbatical I lay awake in my bed in Galveston thinking about Mary's message of prayer and penance. It became clear to me that this is the same teaching of Jesus found in the Scriptures, repeated by our Blessed Mother at Fatima in 1917 and at Medjugorje today. It is the cure for the problems that we face today.

All of a sudden I was filled with a joy that was ecstatic. For a few minutes a bright little light shaped like a dove danced around in my room. I was so scared I began to say my rosary. It seemed like a sign—prayer and penance are the key to peace.

A few weeks later I began to write down the promise I would ask the children to make to Our Lady: to pray, do penance and exercise, to give up some junk food and television.

On this same night about three in the morning, I woke up. It was clear to me: The huge cross on Mount Krizevac was a sign for you and me. The cross of Jesus cures the problems of addictions, overeating or drinking, misuse of TV, drugs and so on. The cross of Jesus is the cure of addiction; prayer and penance are the key.

Once again the Holy Spirit pulled one of his little tricks—a bright blue light appeared in my room. It was in the form of a cross. I was filled with joy and peace.

I share this with you to try to explain why I believe prayer and penance are important to everyone, even to children.

When I returned to Slidell, I gave a talk to the schoolchildren outlining this program of prayer and penance. This took place in the beginning of the school year. A few nights before I had awakened in the middle of the night. I wrote the talk I would give the children. When I returned to bed, I asked Our Lady for a sign of confirmation. The Holy Spirit played his light trick for five minutes. Bright red and green colors played on the ceiling; it looked like a medal of Our Lady. I said the rosary in gratitude. It is nice to know we have a mother who cares and loves us.

I really wish Mary would work some big miracle to show you how important prayer and penance are to you. But for now we have to rely on faith and a very playful Holy Spirit who likes people who are childlike.

Always remember: Peace is Our Blessed Mother's promise to you, but you have to be willing to pay the price. *That price is daily prayer and penance.*

Chapter VI

WITNESS

"You I have appointed a watchman. When you hear me saying anything, you shall warn them for me. If you do not speak out to dissuade the wicked man from his way, I will hold you responsible for his death."

Today each of us is being called by God to be his watchman—to warn the world of the perils of sin and to be witness to the peace that comes from the love of Jesus Christ and his Mother Mary.

While I was in Galveston, I became friends with a kind Jewish doctor. He could not learn enough about our Blessed Mother and Medjugorje. I had to promise that when I returned he would be able to come with me.

He was still smarting over the hurt caused him by a priest many years ago. During the war in Vietnam, he had fallen in love with a beautiful Irish nurse. They wanted to get married and went to see the Catholic chaplain. The chaplain refused to even consider witnessing their marriage. "Go find a good Jewish girl," he was told. Stung by this rebuff, he did eventually meet and marry a Jewish woman. The marriage lasted a very short time. He had a son. When she left him, he wasn't even given their address. "I don't even know where my son lives," he lamented.

This Jewish doctor was intrigued by the apparitions in Medjugorje. He had read that Our Blessed Mother would select one priest to make known the warning to the world when the ten secrets had been revealed to all of the children. "Suppose," he said, "you were the priest. How would you feel?"

I thought about the conversation when I read the warnings by the prophet in Ezekiel, chapter thirty-three. It is the task of each of us to be watchmen—to warn the world that the message of Mary at Medjugorje is both negative as well as positive. We must become by our lives witnesses to that truth: namely, the need for prayer and penance to avoid the perils of which Mary warns us.

The prophet Ezekiel makes it clear that a failure to allow ourselves to be used by the Lord could endanger us as well as those we fail to admonish. It is easy to see that it is no fun to be a prophet.

The positive side is that each of us in our community will become a witness for peace through our penance and our prayer life. Jesus himself assures us of the power of our prayer. "Again I tell you," Jesus says, "if two of you join your voices on earth to pray for anything whatever, it shall be granted you by My Father in heaven. Where two or three are gathered in My name, there am I, in their midst."

Each of us is being called to be a watchman—to warn the world of the dangers of sin and the need for penance. But we are also prophets of joy, calling God's remnant to peace through prayer.

There remains an unanswered question about Medjugorje. We know that the message of Mary conforms to the biblical teachings of the Church. We know it has been the source of great peace for those who visit. We have heard of or seen miraculous events. Are there healings taking place there similar to Lourdes or Fatima?

I would like to share with you the story of Judy Durrant, a wife and mother of four small children, who lives in Calgary, Canada. I received a videotape of her testimony from Imelda Besh, a parishioner of St. Margaret Mary, who went to Medjugorje at the same time as Judy. They became friends. This is Judy's testimony.

On July 17, 1987, Judy Durrant received a call from her doctor. "Judy, you must go into the hospital immediately." Judy had just returned from the doctor's office. "I thought he was calling to say I was pregnant again," the woman recounted.

"Your white blood count is very high," the doctor reported. "Do I have cancer?" she asked. "Yes," he replied. "You have leukemia. You have from three weeks to three years to live." Within two hours, Judy was in a cancer hospital, confirming this diagnosis.

A short time later Judy was told about a tape on Medjugorje. Through the kindness of a man who had recently returned from Yugoslavia, she and her husband watched the tape.

On her next visit her doctor told Judy about the possibility of a bone-marrow transplant. Unfortunately, they could not find a suitable donor from any of her relatives—including her father, mother, uncles, or children. It was not meant to be.

A few months later, Judy woke up. "Dave, don't worry," she told her husband. "I am going to get better." She was convinced it was the Holy Spirit speaking to her these words of encouragement.

On her next visit to the doctor, she told him she wanted to go to Medjugorje. "Why?" the doctor asked.

"I believe I will get better," she replied. For the first time she broke down and cried.

"Go for it," the doctor said. "You must get up every hour while you are on the plane. Otherwise you may have a stroke," he warned.

At Medjugorje Judy and her husband stayed with a couple who had four children. She met the American group, including Imelda Besh.

It was here that Judy met a very gifted priest. During mass he had received a word of encouragement. "Mary is your mother. I have given her to you. She is my mouthpiece. I will not let you go home hungry. I will give each of you a gift."

One of the Franciscan priests prayed over Judy and her husband. "Come back on Friday night." he said. During the healing service that night she experienced a great warmth.

Judy was able to get into the Room of Apparitions twice. The first time she received the message, "Don't worry, your children will be taken care of." Later she was encouraged with the reassurance, "Don't worry, you will be looked after also."

On Friday she went into the Room of Apparitions for the second time. She was quite close to the children. She was already convinced she was healed. She returned to give thanks.

When she went up Mount Krizevac, despite the leukemia, she had no difficulty. When asked later if the climb was difficult, she replied, "It was quite easy." It was obvious to her husband that God was with her on this difficult climb.

Her husband took two pictures of the sun. One picture shows a blue sky with the sun. The film is not affected by the direct sunlight. In the other picture the sky is dark black with a perfect star in the center. This unusual phenomenon of the sun was a little sign of encouragement to Judy and her husband.

When Judy came home, her doctor was amazed. He lowered her medication and told her to return in two weeks. When she returned on December 18, her leukemia was completely cured. She has not had any recurrence since.

An Italian doctor who is spending six months in Yugoslavia at the place of apparitions has received all of Judy's medical records. Her case will be submitted to the Vatican to be used in offical confirmation of these apparitions at Medjugorje. I am sure that each of us might wish to be able to give this powerful testimony of the love and power of Our Blessed Mother in our own lives. But each of us is called to be watchmen—to warn the world of imminent danger if we fail to pray. We are also called to be witnesses to the power of prayer. The message of Medjugorje is a call to prayer and penance. It is also an invitation to peace by a mother who wanted to be remembered by her children not as a grim reaper but as a Queen of Peace.

Watchman and Witness—you are her mouthpiece!

Father Carroll at Mount Krizevac. Beads appear on photo.

Photo of Judy Durrant, who was cured of cancer, and her husband, Dave.

The photograph of the young people in Medjugorje holding the photograph of Our Lady is to show the full color of the original photograph taken by the South American priest before numerous developments and processing faded and cropped it.

The photograph of Our Lady was taken in the small room opposite the sacristy in St. James Church in Medjugorje, Yugoslavia, when the Virgin Mary was appearing to six children. It was taken by a priest from South America. He did not see Our Lady and was very surprised to see her image on the photograph.

The photograph with the small image before the cross was taken on Mount Krizevac in Medjugorje, Yugoslavia. It is believed to be the Blessed Virgin Mary before the cross.

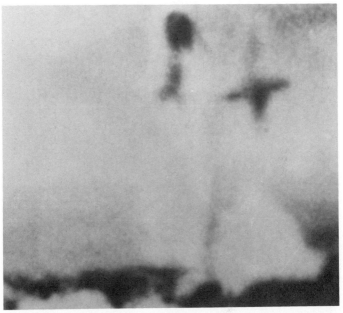

The photograph with the large image beside the cross on Mount Krizevac was taken of the same crowd on the same day (the feast of the Exaltation of the Cross, September 14). It is believed to be Jesus or the Blessed Virgin beside the cross.

The photograph outside the rectory of St. James Church in Medjugorje was taken just minutes before the apparition appeared.

This photo outside the rectory was taken as the apparition was appearing. The cloudiness or mist seen in the photo is felt to be a spirit form, a visible manifestation of the energy it possesses. It is interesting to note that scientists have stated that the level of radiation rises at the time of the apparitions.

Chapter VII

DANIEL, THE DAY OF THE LORD

The apparitions at Medjugorje are clearly apocalyptic elements. The classic apocalyptic elements in the messages are the ten secrets with their implied content of terrible future events, the frequent references to the devil, and the sign promised to appear at Medjugorje. In addition, there have been mysterious signs already witnessed at Medjugorje—strange lights, the sun changing color and moving strangely, visions by large and small groups of people, and healings that demonstrate God's power to save.

There are but few who have not read of the AIDS plague now predicted by the end of this century. It is caused primarily by homosexual or drug activity. Scientists now say that AIDS may be more devastating than the Black Plague that ravaged most of Europe in the fifteenth century. Worldwide 100 to 150 million people may die of AIDS by the turn of the century unless a cure is found shortly.

Scientists say the answer to addiction is education. Teach people "safe sex." One minister handed out condoms in church to demonstrate this point of view.

The answer of the Church is abstinence. Our Blessed Mother adds that the cross of Jesus Christ is the only certain cure: prayer and penance.

To understand the apocalyptic message of Medjugorje we must understand the meaning of the "day of the Lord" in the Bible and discuss the end of the world. To set your minds at ease, it is clear that although we will endure difficult times unless we do penance, the message of Medjugorje is not about the end of the world.

What does the "day of the Lord" mean in the Bible? The Jews and the early Church believed that there was a present day, which is sinful, and the day to come, which will be joyful. In between is the "day of the Lord," which will be a time of great trials. Our Blessed Mother in her apparitions seems to indicate that that time may be near.

If we are to understand this "day of the Lord" that we are facing, we must understand a little of the books of Daniel and Revelation.

Daniel had a dream that terrified him; he wrote it down. He saw four animals: a lion, a bear, a leopard with four heads, and a beast with ten horns and a small horn springing from its midst.

Daniel was using allegorical language familiar to the Jewish people. The idea was simple. Our struggle, like Daniel's, would be against Satan himself. As St. Paul wrote, "The struggle is against principalities and powers." In other words, the power of evil that we will experience is caused by Satan himself.

The good news is more important. The terror of the beast will be broken; the power of God is even greater. At issue for Daniel, the prophet, is the fact that we are in God's hands. This form of storytelling in the Bible is used to conquer the terror of history. It is a way of saying we have been there before, and God will win out for us. The responsibility lies not on our weak shoulders but on God's.

Chapter 7 of Daniel is one of the most powerful in the entire Bible. It draws on symbolism that people understood. It provided the New Testament writer, John, with his most vivid imagery to write the Book of Revelation.

The four beasts in this passage are four kings: the beast like a lion with angel's wings stands for Babylon; the one like a bear stands for Media; the one like a leopard stands for

Persia; and the fourth stands for Alexander the Great.

The ten horns found in Chapter 7 of Daniel represent ten kings. We find this imagery again in Revelation, Chapter 13. The little horn represents Antiochus Ephipanes of Syria. King Epiphanes of Syria overcame the Jews and desecrated the temple in Jerusalem, but his reign would last but three and a half years. According to Daniel, "His allotted time is a time, two times and a half a time." In the end he would be destroyed.

There is little doubt that Daniel helped the Jews to cope with the tragedy of the Syrian king. In the year 167 B.C. King Antiochus Epiphanes, the antichrist, the great Satan, violated the Jewish place of worship, the temple; but Daniel gave them hope. God would prevail over Satan.

In the year 164 B.C. Judas Maccabeus led a rebellion. The Syrians were overcome, the temple of worship was cleansed, and King Antiochus died. Thus through Daniel, God had prepared his people for their "day of the Lord." In the end, God will win.

There was another "day of the Lord," in the first century. In the midst of persecution, John of Patmos wrote the Book of Revelation.

To understand this allegorical book, we must realize that the Church assimilated the Jewish concept of the "day of the Lord"—a period of trial preceding the era of peace. How would this occur? Only God can bring this about. He would destroy the present time and usher in the golden age. The "day of the Lord" would be a terrible time filled with terror and destruction. Apocalyptic literature attempts to explain the unexplainable.

A further complication is the fact that John was writing at a time of persecution. Since the enemies of Christianity would view this writing as revolutionary, it is written in a code hard to decipher.

What is the meaning of the beasts in Revelation? There

are two beasts in this New Testament writing: the beast from the sea with the ten horns and seven heads; the second beast comes out of the earth with two horns to promote the interest of the beast.

Satan, the devil, has been cast out of heaven. He is determined to do as much damage as he is able. He delegates his power to two beasts, who are key figures in the story. The first is the beast from the sea; he stands for the Roman Empire. John borrowed this image from Daniel chapter 7. John embellished the story by taking elements from all four of Daniel's beasts to describe Rome, so evil did the early Church writer consider that empire.

The beast of Revelation has seven heads and ten horns. These stand for the emperors of Rome. Since the first emperor, Augustus, there were Tiberius, Caligula, Claudius, Nero Vespasian, Titus, and Domitian. These are the heads.

The beast had ten horns. After Nero's death, there was a short period of complete chaos. During the following eighteen months, Galba, Otho, and Vitellius ruled. They are not included in the seven heads but are listed among the horns.

We have seen that the first beast empowered by Satan was the Roman Empire. The second beast, "the beast from the land," is the provincial organization of rulers and priesthoods that enforced Caesar's worship. Nero called himself the "savior of the world." Later emperors took the name *Dominus*, the *Lord*, a title reserved in the New Testament for Jesus Christ alone. The name *God* was used by the emperors. The second beast enforced this Caesar or divine worship of the emperors; Christians had the choice of saying Caesar is Lord or dying.

Two savage beasts, the might of Rome and its organization of Caesar worship, oppressed early Christians. What little hope did they have? They had the power of God himself.

During the Roman persecution of the first century, a legend arose that the dreaded Nero had actually resurrected.

This was the Nero-resurrected belief. So fierce were these persecutions of the Christians at that time that the emperors became the antichrist—the Satan revived. Few people in history evoked the terror of Nero.

Nero reigned as emperor from A.D. 55 to 68. Nero was fathered by Cnaeus Domitius Ahenobarbus, who was known for his wickedness. Ahenobarbus killed another who refused to drink wine with him. He had deliberately run over a child with his chariot. He had gouged out the eye of a Roman soldier. He died a fearsome death.

Nero's mother was Agrippina. When Nero was three, she was banished by Emperor Caligula. Nero was cared for by an aunt, Lepida, who gave him over to two wretched slaves, one a barber and the other a dancer, to raise.

When she was recalled from exile, Agrippina had but one desire: to make her son emperor. When Nero was eleven, she married Emperor Claudius, even though she knew he was her uncle. She had him adopt Nero as a son. The great scholar Seneca was summoned to tutor the boy.

After five years Agrippina poisoned her husband. As soon as he died, Nero was led forth as the new emperor. His mother had bribed the army on his behalf.

Shortly afterward, Nero murdered Britannicus, the rightful heir to the throne. Nero was a blatant homosexual who married Sporus in a state wedding and took him on a bridal tour of Greece. Nero also married a free man called Doryphorus. He took Poppaea Sabina, the wife of Otho, his closest friend, as a lover and killed her when he learned she was pregnant.

In the year A.D. 64, the great fire of Rome occurred. Historians believe that either Nero caused the fire or refused to allow it to be put out. The fire burned a week. He blamed the fire on the Christians and intensified their persecution.

Nero repeatedly tried to kill his own mother. When the senate finally declared him a public enemy, he committed suicide. You can understand how the early Christians thought of him as evil incarnate. This is the reason that later persecutions of the Church seemed to be evil revisited. Hence the origin of the legend of the "head wounded and restored."

In chapter 20 of Revelation, the resolution of the "day of the Lord" is found: "Then I saw an angel come down from heaven holding the key to the abyss and a huge chain in his hand. He seized the dragon, the ancient serpent who is the devil or Satan, and chained him up for a thousand years. The angel hurled him into the abyss which he closed and sealed over him.

"Then I saw some thrones; they came to life again and reigned with Christ for a thousand years."

The Book of Revelation was intended by John to be a message of hope. Embroiled as they were in persecution, the early Church seemed to be overwhelmed by evil.

John, just as Daniel before him in the Old Testament, gave the survivors hope. Look to the end and see: It is God's world; you will overcome; the prize will be yours—peace in this life and eternal life in heaven.

In our own day, we will experience frightening events. At times we may feel overwhelmed by evil. The Bible clearly teaches us the need to rely on God alone; He is in charge. Fear not, little ones. Jesus promised to be with us always until the end of time. Love casts out fear, and you are a community of lovers.

In the midst of terrifying events, we must realize that it is God's world; we are in His hands. The Book of Revelation tells us how to handle the fear of the "day of the Lord"—trust in Jesus Christ alone.

The Book of Revelation ends like this: "The one who gives this testimony says, 'Yes, I am coming soon. Amen. Come, Lord Jesus. The grace of the Lord Jesus be with you all. Amen.' "

Chapter VIII

THE PLAGUES

The message of Medjugorje is clearly apocalyptic. Our Blessed Mother indicated that these will be her final visits to the world. Mary has pleaded for prayer and penance and warned that a failure to heed her direction will result in major trials. These trials have a familiar ring. Perhaps this is the "day of the Lord" predicted in the Bible.

What does the Bible say about the "day of the Lord"? The Jews as well as the early Christians considered the "day of the Lord" a frightening time. For John, author of the Book of Revelation, it was a time of universal terror. He was giving us a picture with which the Jews would be quite familiar. When the "day of the Lord" came, men would be afraid. In the Old Testament Zephania said, "The mighty would cry." Joel said, "The inhabitants would tremble." Enoch wrote there would be no place to hide. God would be a witness against his sinful people, according to Micah. "Who could endure it?" ask Joel. Jesus himself, on the way to the cross, recalled the words of Hosea, "Men would say to the mountains, 'cover us' and to the hills, 'fall on us.' "

The day of the Lord would, according to the prophets, involve an upheaval of the universe. Relations would be destroyed; hatred would reign supreme. According to Enoch, parents would hate their own children; from dawn to dusk they would murder them; honor would be turned into shame and strength into humiliation, beauty into ugliness. Baruch said passion would hold sway over the man who was once peaceful. "Who can endure the day of his coming? Sinners," said Enoch, "would be destroyed."

Let us look at the Book of Revelation to see what the "day of the Lord" may be like. We must remember that it is difficult to understand because this book was written in allegorical style, designed to confuse the Roman persecutors.

In Revelation 13:5 John says of Satan, "The beast was allowed to wage war against God's people and conquer them." In this century Satan has attacked God's people in two ways: (1) through Communism, which professes no belief in God, and (2) through unbridled materialism in the West, where while paying lip service to God, people have made money, sex, and power their god.

During this century Communism has enslaved one and a half billion people. In the West we have come to act as if God is dead; disbelief is rampant.

The Book of Revelation describes the "day of wrath" as seven plagues. Let us see what this text meant to John and imagine what these plagues could mean if the world fails to pray and do penance as Our Blessed Mother warned.

In chapter 16 of Revelation the angels are given the task of pouring out God's wrath on the world. We are told, "The first angel poured out his bowl on the earth—severe and festering boils."

For the writer of the Apocalypse, the first terror is a plague of malignant and ulcerous sores. The word is the same used to describe the boils during the plagues in Egypt.

I believe this plague may well be that of AIDS. Six months ago a paper made the following prediction: "A worldwide AIDS epidemic will become so serious it will dwarf such earlier medical disasters as the Black Plague, smallpox and typhoid. The nation's health chief, Bowen, said, 'There is no known cure, 50 million to 100 million people worldwide could contract the AIDS virus in the next two decades. Between 1 million and 1.5 million Americans are now believed to be carrying the virus.' "

The second plague in Revelation: "The sea turned to blood like a corpse and every creature in the sea dies." John used the plague reminiscent of the waters of the Nile turned into blood by Moses.

Recently it was reported that a red tide had affected the Gulf area from Padre Island for a hundred miles. Dead fish washed up upon the beaches. On the east coast hundreds of dolphins, the smartest of the sea creatures, have died in the Atlantic. The scientists have no idea what caused these deaths. For people who depend upon the sea for food, it is easy to see how this plague could be frightening.

The third angel, according to Revelation, "poured out his bowl on the rivers and springs. These turned to blood."

The explanation of this plague is contained in verse 6. John says. "To those who shed the blood of the saints and prophets, you have given blood to drink; they deserve it."

John is referring to the blood of the early Christian martyrs killed in Rome. The leaders of the Church were the first to suffer persecution.

This plague should warn us that the price of dedication to Christ has always been persecution.

Certainly the fear of contaminated water can cause great concern. We know that the government is presently planning to spend 20 billion dollars to try to clean up water contaminated by pollution.

There was a story about a small town, Bynum, North Carolina, where 59 percent of the people who died since 1975 had cancer caused by contaminated drinking water.

The fourth plague foretold was fire. The fourth angel was commissioned to "burn men with fire." John tells us, "Those who were scorched blasphemed the name of God, but they did not repent." St. Paul, writing to the Romans, gave this fearful omen: "Even when men know that sin causes God's punishment, they are not likely to change."

The fourth plague reminds us of some of the evils of our day. We are told by medical experts that in abortions the fetus can in some instances experience pain. The sensation that a developed fetus, which is aborted by chemicals, feels is a burning sensation.

We know how tragic war is to mankind. The statistics in the 1986 *World Almanac* show that we had 25,324 casualties in the Revolutionary War, 498,332 in the Civil War, 116,708 in World War I, 497,316 in World War II, 54,246 in the Korean War, 58,655 in the Vietnam War. Since 1973, when abortions were legalized, we have had 19,500,000 abortions in the United States alone.

I imagine when the prophet warned that parents would kill their own children from dawn to dusk, the people must have thought him mad. Yet today it is coming to pass.

The fourth plague may well be that of legalized murder. This plague may also involve drugs, particularly alcohol and cocaine. The experts say that in our country drugs are now at epidemic levels. Despite the tremendous efforts on the part of government, the misuse of recreational drugs is no longer under control. Six million people are addicted to cocaine.

The fifth plague was one of darkness. "Men bit their tongues in pain and blasphemed the God of heaven because of their sufferings and boils," John tells us, "but they did not turn from their wicked deeds."

The fifth plague could easily remind us of the sexual sins of our times. It is said that there are twenty million Americans afflicted with genital herpes, which is currently incurable. The gift of sex has been taken out of the context of marriage and misused.

According to the Census Bureau, unmarried-couple households have increased by 1 million since 1980, totaling 2.6 million last year. The report said 15.3 million children under eighteen lived with one parent last year, an increase of nearly 3 million since 1980. Of that number, 4.7 million children under eighteen in single-parent homes lived with a parent who had never married.

When you see the epidemic of divorce rampant today, you must also wonder if Satan had a hand in this. When love begins to die in a society, darkness rules. Five and nine-tenths million children under eighteen live with a divorced parent, 3.2 million with a separated parent, and 3.8 million with a married parent whose spouse was absent.

The sixth plague occurred when "the angel poured out his bowl on the great river Euphrates. Its water was dried up to prepare the way for the kings of the East."

In the Old Testament the drying up of the waters is a sign of the power of God. It happened at the Red Sea when Moses crossed. Joshua also passed over the Jordan by drying up the river.

It is possible that John is remembering a famous incident in history: When Cyrus the Persian captured Babylon, he did it by drying up the Euphrates. The river flows through the center of the city. Cyrus had a brilliant plan: He deflected the course of the river into a lake. The level of the river dropped, and the channel of the river through Babylon became a dry road. The Persians gained entry into Babylon and the city fell.

The drying up of water could remind us of the problem of hunger. The pictures from Africa of hundreds of thousands off people dying of starvation certainly show the makings of a plague. They have also shown pictures on TV of locusts that have eaten thousands of acres of land, another cause of starvation.

Perhaps the greatest plague that this reminds me of is loneliness. When love dries up, people turn to despair. Many of the people who commit suicide are terribly lonely people.

The final plague was "poured out of the empty air; lightning, thunder and earthquakes followed; mountains disappeared, hailstones came crashing to earth."

The devastating hail was part of the plagues of Egypt. In the battle of Beth-Horon under Joshua, there was a great hailstorm. More were killed by the hail then by the sword. Finally, Ezekiel speaks of God pleading with men through pestilence and blood and of using great hailstones, fire, and brimstone.

The seventh plague could certainly come through the pollution of the air. One of the great fears of nuclear war would be the effect on the atmosphere. We also know the pollution from factories could easily become a plague. Acid rain has already been seen as a fearful omen. The destruction of the ozone layer by fluorocarbons could become a catastrophe. Scientists openly worry about the hole in the ozone, which is widening near the Arctic Circle. Earthquakes and volcanos certainly pose great dangers.

When we think of the awesome power of God, we realize that these plagues are meant to be a warning, a call by God to change our lives.

When we read that Mary is warning us through the children in Yugoslavia to do penance and pray to avoid trials, we must take her seriously. Read the Book of Revelation and recognize that the "day of the Lord" will be a time of great trial.

But the Book of Revelation was written to be a message of hope for the Christian people threatened with despair.

The Book of Revelation ends like this: "The one who gives this testimony says, 'Yes, I am coming soon. Amen. Come, Lord Jesus. The grace of the Lord Jesus be with you all. Amen.' "

The author of Revelation prayed for the coming of Jesus Christ. John firmly placed his trust in Christ. You notice the Bible ends with grace. Our survival through the "day of the Lord" is totally dependent on the grace of Jesus Christ. It is encouraging to remember the promise of Jesus, that He would be with us until the end of time. Our confidence is in Him alone.

Chapter IX

THE END OF THE WORLD

There are two reasons to believe that the end of the world is near. Our Blessed Mother said that the apparitions at Medjugorje would be her final appearance on the earth. According to the prophecies of Malachy, there will only be two popes to follow the present pontiff, John Paul II.

The prophesies of Malachy are most interesting. Historians are in agreement that they were not written by Malachy, who lived from 1095 to 1148. They were actually a forgery, published in 1594 by an unknown writer. Because Malachy was famous for prophecy during his lifetime, his name was used. But we have to admit some of his predictions were uncanny.

Each prediction consists of two or three words in Latin that refer to each pope. Among the most significant are the following:

Montium Custos, Guardian of the Hills: Alexander VII (1655–67) had as his family crest three hills with a star above them.

Rosa Umbriae, the Rose of Umbria: Clement XIII (1758–69) served in Umbria before he became Pope Umbrias. His emblem was a rose.

Ursus Velox, Swift Bear: Clement XIV (1769–74) had the image of a running bear on his family crest.

Peregrinus Apostolicus, Apostolic Wanderer: Pius VI (1755–99) spent the last years of his life as a fugitive from the political aftermath of the French Revolution.

De Balneis Etruria, From the Baths of Etruria: Gregory XVI (1831–45) held office in Etruria before his election.

Religio Depopuilata, Religion Laid Waste: The pope to whom this applied in the sequence of prophecy was Benedict XV (1914–20), whose reign spanned World War I and the subsequent world influenza epidemic.

Pastor Angelicus, The Angelic Shepherd: Pius XII (1939–58) was a devoted student of St. Thomas Aquinas, traditionally known as the Angelic Doctor.

Pastor et Nauta, Shepherd and Navigator: John XXIII (1958–63) was a shepherd and navigator of the Second Vatican Council.

Flos Floruum, Flower of Flowers: Paul VI (1963–78) had the fleur-de-lis as his personal coat of arms.

De Mediate Luna, From the Half Moon: This refers to Pope John Paul I. He was elected pope on August 26, 1978. He died thirty-three days later, on September 28, 1978, approximately in the middle of the lunar month marked by the full moons of September 16 and October 16.

The present pope, John Paul II, who was elected in 1978, is called *De Labore Solis*, From the Toil of the Sun. The meaning of this is not clear. However, anyone who has been present at one of his outdoor masses such as the one in New Orleans must wonder how he endures the heat. It would surprise no one if his death occurs because of a heat stroke.

The two remaining popes are signified as *De Gloria Olivae*, the Glory of the Olive, and *Petrus Romanus*, Peter of Rome. Incidentally, there has only been one Pope Peter, and that was the head of the apostles and the first pope.

Some believe that Rome will be destroyed and the final judgment will come during the reign of Peter.

I personally believe that we must be prepared to endure some of the trials associated with "day of the Lord" alluded to in the Book of Revelation. In our Blessed Mother's apparitions to the children at Medjugorje, she told them that this was the century of the Devil. She also indicated that his time to exercise his power is growing short; and consequently, the trials in the next few years will be very intense.

In view of the fact that Our Blessed Mother indicated that her apparitions at Medjugorje were to be her last, does that mean the end of the world is near? The answer is clearly no. Our Blessed Mother Herself cautioned against those prophets of doom who simply frightened people. At Medjugorje Mary was asked by the children about these dire predictions concerning the end of the world. This is what she told them on October 21, 1983: "This comes from false prophets," she said. "They say, 'on such a day at such a time there will be a catastrophe.' I have always said the evil (punishment) will come if the world is not converted. Call people to conversion. Everything depends on your conversion."

In my judgment, the "day of the Lord" will soon be experienced. Mary told the children in Yugoslavia that the final two messages, which are punishments, will occur. They may be lessened by prayer and penance, but they will happen.

This series of punishment will give way to great peace. If we persevere during this difficult period, we will see a great period of peace. One of the key elements in Mary's message at Fatima in 1917 was that with penance and prayer this time of wrath can be shortened. She promised that if we do this and Russia is consecrated to her Immaculate Heart, Russia will be converted and a great period of peace will be enjoyed by the world.

These two things will occur before the end of the world: the conversion of Russia and a period of great peace. When asked by the children who she was, our Blessed Mother responded, "Queen of Peace." The message of Mary at Medjugorje was one of peace, not of damnation or the end of the world. When you hear that a pope who takes the name of Peter II, you will have a clear sign "the day of the Lord" is over; a great period of peace is to begin.

Nevertheless, even though the end of the world is not near, we cannot relax our prayer or penance. It is clear that Mary was warning us at Medjugorje that although the century of the devil is drawing to a close, Satan will pull out all of the stops.

You, my dear brothers and sisters, will be part of the remnant. You will survive the crisis of faith and the perils of the "day of the Lord" because of your commitment to prayer and your willingness to do penance. From the youngest to the oldest, we must understand that penance and prayer are essential.

I believe that the trials of the "day of the Lord" will be addictions. It is the cross of Jesus Christ alone that can cure addiction. When these addictions become plagues, many will cry out that the end of the world is near. The remnant alone will know that this is not true. It is simply the time of testing foretold in the Book of Revelation. Our Blessed Mother warned us at Fatima and now at Medjugorje. The cure is the cross of Jesus Christ.

During the struggle, when you are frightened, turn to the final prayer that ends the Bible with the Book of Revelation. It goes like this: "The one who gives this testimony says, 'Yes, I am coming soon. Amen. Come, Lord Jesus. The grace of the Lord Jesus be with you all. Amen.' "

You should see in these words of revelation written by John, at the height of Roman persecution in the first century, the cause of our hope—Jesus Christ alone. Place your confidence in Him. If the end of the world was near, our Blessed Mother would have warned us. She would not have chosen to call herself the Queen of Peace.

But make no mistake about it: The price of peace is the cross. Prayer and penance are the key.

Chapter X

RETURN TO MEDJUGORJE

On June 25, 1988, the seventh anniversary of our Blessed Mother's appearances at Medjugorje was celebrated. I had the uneasy feeling that Joseph's seven years of plenty were over and the seven lean years were about to begin. The Mississippi River is drying up; the plague of AIDS, addictions to drugs, illicit sex, homosexuality, and alcohol are fearful omens.

My second pilgrimage to Medjugorje began on June 11 at 9:00 A.M. A group of thirty-eight departed nonstop to New York. We were to be joined by the Danons from Florida, Mrs. Patton and Mrs. Standrige from Memphis.

We arrived at La Guardia and were bused to JFK. At JFK we learned that the flight was overbooked. Anthony Hymel, my brother-in-law, and I presented our reserved tickets and did our best to keep the seats for our four missing members. The ticket clerk promised to try. While we were in line, one man was told that he had no reservation. "What about my bags?" he asked as the bags were about to go on the conveyor belts. "Your bags can go to Yugoslavia if you wish," the clerk retorted, "but you may not."

Four people from Florida, the Meyers, were bumped by the travel agent. They left a day earlier than we did and joined us in Rome. We arrived in Rome Tuesday after a connecting flight from Kennedy to Belgrade.

On Wednesday we attended a papal audience. Carol Darby, a disabled parishioner, had her motorized scooter with her. Deacon Henry Zeringue accompanied Carol to a front-row seat for the audience. They both were privileged to shake hands with the pope.

Wednesday afternoon our group toured Rome. Although it was intended as a free day, because the Meyers would have to leave Rome a day early, our plans were changed. Many were exhausted.

Thursday morning, my brother, Father Ralph Carroll, and I celebrated mass with our group in the crypt of St. Peter's. We were supposed to use the chapel of St. Peter's near the first pope's tomb; but despite our reservations, another group was there. We ended up at a shrine to our Blessed Mother. It meant a great deal to me, since the words on the back wall surrounding Mary were *Maria, sub tuum praesidium confugimus*, "Mary, under your protection we flee." This will be on the banner of the remnant church during the day of the Lord.

After mass I found a rest room in the priest sacristy. A few minutes later, as we prepared to leave St. Peter's, I discovered I had lost my wallet and traveler's checks. I fled to the sacristy to learn they had found my things. They sent me to the front of the church accompanied by an altar boy who spoke perfect English.

After a few minutes, it was clear that red tape would delay me. The group went to the Vatican Museum and the Sistine Chapel, as my altar boy led me to an administration building outside the church. Fifteen minutes later, I had retrieved my wallet. Our Blessed Mother knew I needed the rest and allowed me this extra time to myself.

I rejoined the group at lunch. We had an afternoon tour, which ended somewhat early because our group was physically drained.

Thursday night my brother, Father Ralph, the two nuns from Slidell (Sister Donna and Sister Mary Ann), June Walker, a parishioner, and I went to the Piccalo Mondo, a great Italian restaurant.

Friday morning we were free from the group. We visited the top of St. Peter's, went shopping, had a wild Roman taxi ride, and packed to leave for Yugoslavia.

Once again, it was hurry and wait. From Rome we flew to Belgrade, from Belgrade to Dubrovnick. We arrived late Friday night at the Platka Hotel.

After breakfast on Saturday we went by motorcoach to Medjugorje, a three-hour bus ride. At Medjugorje we divided up into five houses.

There were twelve in our little family: the two nuns, Carol and her mother, my sister Yvonne, Anthony, her husband, my niece Angele, June Walker, Father Ralph, and I. It was a great gift to get to know the nuns a little better as human beings, and not religious sterotypes. I teased the nuns about being called "good sisters or little nuns." This couldn't apply to Mary Ann, who is five-nine.

On Saturday night we were priviledged to see Ivan, one of the visionaries. He was interviewed by a group of young people from New Orleans. Father Calkins, son of a St. Margaret Mary parishioner, was present that night.

On Sunday we went to the English mass at 12:15 P.M. and the Croatian mass at 7:00 P.M. The rosary was recited at 6:00 P.M.

Monday morning I celebrated mass with Father Ralph in the Chapel of Apparitions. This is a small sacristy room on the right side of the church. Forty-seven crowded into the room. This room had been used during the early apparitions. The first appearance was on the hillside. Because of government opposition, they were moved to the sacristy. Next they were held in a rectory office. Last year they were moved to the choir loft of St. James Church, and no one is allowed to be present during the apparition. After mass Carmel took us to see Vicka. I was most impressed by her sense of calm. There is a constant pressure from pilgrims wishing to see her. After waiting quite a while, Vicka appeared and spoke for a few minutes.

"Reread the message of Our Lady," she said. "Peace, prayer, fasting, and the rosary were stressed. Our Lady wants you to give up one thing you really like, but most of all, give up sinning." We were all moved by her simplicity and serenity. Most of us reached out and touched her hand.

Our group then went up the Hill of Apparitions to the Blue Cross. This is a small cross a short way up the Hill of Apparitions often used by the children's prayer group. Even Carol was able to accompany us on this climb. Sister Mary Grace insisted we go there.

Monday afternoon I went into the Room of Apparitions with Father Ralph and my cousin Jim Carroll. After some time I learned it was Father Slavko who gave permission for entrance to the choir loft, the place of apparitions; but Father Slavko has a look-alike Franciscan priest. After several efforts I finally met Father Slavko.

"Father, my cousin Jim works for Channel 6 and would like to tape the apparitions," I said. "Also, Archbishop Hannon has a program once a week on Medjugorje. He may be able to use the film."

"One person only may go," Father Slavko replied. "Only one person. Come ten minutes to six. I will let one person in," he said.

At 5:30 P.M. Jim, Ralph, and I arrived at the base of the stairs. We were carrying the thousand rosaries I had brought from Slidell. I saw the nun who runs the sacristy. "I am waiting for Father Slavko," I told her. "We have permission to film the apparitions." I didn't lie—we did have permission. I was using the majestic "we."

"Come in, but hurry," she said. Ralph had half of the rosaries, which weighed about seventy-five pounds. Once inside, Ralph decided since he didn't have permission he was going to leave the choir loft. He walked down the stairs, only to find he was locked in. He didn't want to be disobedient, so he tried to leave but couldn't. He went in simply to carry the rosaries.

The strange thing is that he was looking for a sign, as he later shared. He didn't want to be in the room and tried to leave. Was it a sign that Mary wanted Ralph there? I certainly think so. There were more than a hundred priests at Medjugorje who wanted to be in the apparitions room, but he was chosen.

At six o'clock Father Slavko came into the choir loft with Ivan, the only visionary who would be present. Two Franciscans, a nun, and a child who had also slipped in were present. Father Slavko went up to Ralph to ask him what we were doing in the choir loft. He then remembered, came over to me, and said, "I remember—you can stay."

The apparition experience taught me an important lesson. Ralph had taken one of the two kneelers in the choir loft. When Ivan entered, he offered it to him; but the visionary politely refused and sat on a bench on one side of me. Father Slavko sat on a bench on the other side and seemed to fall asleep. We prayed the rosary with the people in the church downstairs.

I judged that the visionary didn't look very pious—manly, but not pious. And why didn't he kneel on the hard marble floor for the rosary? Visionaries should look pious. . . .

At 6:39 P.M. Ivan got up and quietly knelt in front of a statue of Mary, which is near the rear wall. We all fell to our knees. The apparition lasted perhaps five minutes. The people, unlike in the past, continued to pray the rosary.

Ivan then got up and left the choir with Father Slavko. I followed close behind. "Did Mary say anything special?" I asked. Father Slavko translated. "No," was the dull reply.

Jim was really shaken. Later he would explain that during

the apparition Ivan's eyes seemed to move, distracted toward the camera. He wasn't in a trance. Ralph and I asked him to wait before passing judgment. "I don't want to do anything to discourage the faith of the people," he replied.

Jim got the rosaries home by cab; Ralph and I went to mass. Here the Lord convicted me of my judgmental attitude.

I have mentioned to my parishioners that I have been blind in my right eye since I was twenty-two. A cure for my blindness was uppermost in my prayers. The gospel that night was read in English by my brother, Ralph. He felt being asked was his sign. The gospel is read in five or six languages. That night the gospel really hit home—it was on judging. Jesus says, "If you have a plank in your eye, take the plank out before you try to take the speck out of your brother's eye."

Here I am, blind in one eye, complaining that the visionary didn't look holy, didn't kneel during the rosary. Yet I am privileged to offer the Eucharist each day, and I often say Mass in such a hurry, as I am anxious to leave. What right did I have to judge my brother Ivan?

Tuesday morning most of our group went up Mount Krisevac. We recited the stations in three small groups going up the mountain. It took an hour and twenty minutes for the first contingent to reach the top. A few of our number met a sergeant major in the United States army. He told how someone in their group had seen the cross on Mount Krisevac turn gold during the day; it later turned red. Later I learned that Deacon Henry had seen the cross turn gold during the gospel one day when he was being crowded out of the church during mass. He looked up to the mountain; the cross was gold.

Tuesday afternoon about four-thirty I went over to the church to say the rosary and get a cup of coffee. I saw Father Gallagher and invited him to our going-away party. Around five I moved to the outside statue in the plaza in front of the church. As I was saying my rosary, the clouds seemed to part.

The sun came out strong. The miracle of the sun appeared like a host with colored rays emanating from it. I thanked the Lord, but, fearful for my one good eye, I went back to prayer.

I was most appreciative that despite the trauma of leading a large tour with Anthony and all the problems we had encountered, I had a sense of peace.

At 6:30 P.M. I began to look up at the two front windows, which have white frosted glass. I now knew where the visionary would be positioned.

At 6:40 P.M. I began to look up to see a light emanating from the choir loft. It was similar to the light from a movie projector, yet much softer. It was almost like a cloud. It lasted perhaps five minutes. I knew in faith our Blessed Mother was present.

Then the window above the visionary's head became colored like a stained-glass window. I thought at one moment it might be the Sacred Heart. The whole experience lasted perhaps ten minutes.

Was it real? Is Mary really coming to Medjugorje? To the person of faith there is no doubt; to one without it, no amount of proof will suffice. Signs are not meant for proof; they prove nothing without faith. Many return from Medjugorje feeling cheated: they thought they paid for a miracle and did not receive it.

The trip back the next day to Dubrovnick was uneventful. Finally, on Thursday, June 23, we boarded an early flight from Dubrovnick to Belgrade. Shortly after noon we left for New York. I changed my watch to local New York time. We were to land at 3:40 P.M. Eastern Standard Time. Forty minutes before we landed, my niece kept checking the time. My watch was working fine.

Despite incredible hardship we managed to get our group on the return flight at 6:11 P.M. from the Eastern terminal. In the process my baggage was delayed a day, the people from

Memphis missed their flight, and my watch changed. The face on my watch turned completely around on its own. The stem is now on the left side of the face, instead of the right. It is weird! Sister Mary Grace had warned of the presence of Satan. Was he at work on my watch?

Our group finally landed Thursday night in New Orleans after a stop in Atlanta. We were thoroughly exhausted.

Friday night, before I went over for the Prayer Group Mass, I said one decade of the rosary. The cross and the center medallion seemed to turn a different color. The center medallion is Christ holding the chalice and host: the sign of adoration and the Eucharist, which are so important to this community. The next day another rosary had red on the crucifix and medalion of Mary. The two crucifixes I bought from the Franciscan monastery seemed to be gold colored. What does all of this mean to me?

I learned something important about signs. Believe first and signs will follow; but if you ask for a sign as a price of belief, you will come away disillusioned.

Don't judge! Visionary, priest, parishioner, or your own child. Value comes not from ourselves. We are all channels of the grace and love of Jesus Christ. Don't esteem the messenger, cherish the message and the grace of Jesus Christ.

Don't be afraid to share your signs with others.

Don't try to manipulate God; I am great at this. I wanted Him to heal my blindness; He wants to heal our lack of self-love.

Love your children and show it. A woman who conceived outside of wedlock told me she hated her daughter. When she looked at her, she saw nothing but sin. I met her eleven-year-old child in Medjugorje and told her, "You are an absolutely beautiful child." She melted because she knew the message did not come from her but from Mary and Jesus. All because her mother could not tell her own daughter, "I love you."

Love yourself; forgive yourself. Mary used me to heal a woman who had been sexually abused repeatedly by her father when she was a child. Mary sent word to me through one of our groups—she was cured.

Mary promised a permanent sign. I believe the cross may prove to be a sign. I told you of two people who saw the cross as gold and later as red. Tuesday night before we left Medjugorje, a group of us saw a light around the cross. It appeared to be a neon sign lighting up the cross, which is made of concrete. The ones who believed saw this as a sign; the others said it must be a candle or a flashlight or something.

Is it real? Signs are like love: They are in the eye of the beholder.

Signs will never prove Mary appears in Yugoslavia. To those who believe, they will see signs. Even those who believe may question what they have seen. I saw it, but it can't be true, they say to themselves.

I believe we are soon to enter the period of trials foretold by Mary. You have been given an antedote by our Blessed Mother—prayer and fasting. The cross is the cure of addiction. "Just as the serpent in the desert was lifted up," Jesus said, "so too will the son of man be lifted up."

Regardless what the trials may be, you, my dear children, have the protection of our Blessed Mother. "Mary, under your protection we flee."

Chapter XI

THE GOLD CROSS

Following the sermon on the "Return to Medjugorje" at the 8:30 A.M. mass the first Sunday after my return from Medjugorje, I was confronted by Dr. Neal Faciane. "Friday night," he said, "three children who had attended the prayer group were looking up at the moon. Their ages are six, seven, and eleven. They all saw something special." Neal separated the children and asked them to draw what they saw. Below is a report of what these children witnessed.

"First we were playing outside. My dad directed my head toward the moon. The moon had a cross on it. It was red, but it turned gold. I was amazed. I told Colleen and Elisha. Then angels were flying around the moon and there was a halo. They were amazed too."

"The first scene was a cross flashing different colors. The cross was all red, then all gold, then green in the middle at times."

The children also saw a chalice, which was gold and silver. They saw the host, which was white.

The children saw two hills at Medjugorje, one larger than the other. Two of the three children saw Father Carroll under the larger hill, which had a huge cross. The cross was red, then it turned gold.

It seems to me the most significant thing is the cross—red at one time, later gold. This confirms my feeling that the cross is a sign promised by our Blessed Mother. The cross at Medjugorje was seen as red and as gold. Many pilgrims at Medjugorje have seen the light around the cross, which looks like a neon sign.

I mentioned earlier that two silver colored crosses that I purchased at a Franciscan monastery near Medjugorje turned to a goldlike color.

I returned to Slidell after a brief visit with some friends in Houston. After my first trip to Medjugorje I was sent two copies of a print taken in front of the cross on Mount Krisevac: the rosary beads appeared on the print, which was the reason the pictures were sent to me. After returning in July, I found the two pictures had changed: one had a red hue to it, the other gold. But what could the red and gold cross mean?

I believe the red cross signifies the trials that we will soon experience. The gold cross is a promise: that peace promised by our Blessed Mother would eventually occur. The three children in Slidell heard two words—peace and love.

The message of our Blessed Mother on June 25, 1988, may well be her plea to endure the trials that will come, keeping our eyes on the promised peace.

"Dear children, I am calling you to that love which is loyal and pleasing to God. Little children's love bears everything, bitter and difficult for the sake of Jesus, who is love. Therefore, dear children, pray that God comes to your aid; however, not according to your desires, but according to this love. Surrender yourself to God so that He may heal you, console you, and forgive everything inside you which is a hindrance on the way of love. In this way God can move your life and you will grow in love. Dear children, glorify God with a hymn of love so that God's love may be able to grow in you day by day to its fullness. Thank you for having responded to my call."

One final word: I believe the "day of the Lord" is about to begin. Our Blessed Mother has encouraged us for seven years to pray, to fast. Trials Mary warned would occur; they could be lessened but not taken away. It seems to me that these trials are soon to be upon us, but the final word of Mary is peace. Many return seeking that peace that the world cannot give.

Each pilgrim who visits Medjurgorje becomes a sign of peace. Each of us possesses a small part of our Blessed Mother's message. She has touched each of us and given us that peace.

But peace comes at a price. For Jesus Christ it meant suffering and dying on the cross. The cross today is also our sign, not only of redemption but the cure for the addictions that will occur during the "day of the Lord."

Jesus himself used this timely example: The Jews suffering from the poisonous bites of serpents in the desert were being punished by God for their sinfulness. Upon the entreaty of the people of God, Moses prayed for relief. God told Moses to make a golden serpent. Those who looked at it would be spared. Jesus, using this imagery, told us, "Just as the serpent was lifted up in the desert, so too will the son of man be lifted up." It is Jesus lifted up on the cross who will save us from sin. It is the cross of Christ that will be the sign in our time of struggle. The cross alone cures the addictions of sin.

Medjugorje, however, is about peace. It has brought peace to countless people through repentance. Mary's message will bring us through our trials to the great time of peace. When asked by what title she should be called, she responded, "Queen of Peace." It is my hope that this message of our Blessed Mother will be a source of peace for each of you and your families.

CONCLUSION

It began just over eight years ago—Mary, the mother of Jesus, appearing to children in Medjugorje, Yugoslavia. The warning was clear and apocalyptic: repent, do penance and pray; trials will soon come upon the world. These chastisements can be lessened but not eliminated.

The signs are clearly present. Is this the dreaded "day of the Lord" predicted in the Bible? Scientists warned that AIDS is a plague equal in intensity to the Black Plague of the Middle Ages. Genital herpes is epidemic. Sexual sins, from illicit sex to homosexuality, proliferate. A million and a half abortions a year occur in the United States. Addictions have become modern man's scourge. The pleadings of Our Blessed Mother are going unheeded and the drug war is declared lost.

Even Mother Earth has begun a plea for survival. The midwest suffered its worst drought since the 1930s. The red tide has caused massive fish kills in the Gulf. The beaches on the East and West coasts have begun to sport the paraphernalia of death—drug needles and garbage. Wholesale deaths of seals in the North Sea show pollution to be a worldwide calamity; and experts question if the AIDS-like virus in these mammals would next afflict mankind.

The greed of men has gone unabated. Massive wealth has been accumulated through corporate raiding, raising theft of industry to a level that demands college credits in prestigious universities. Insider trading elevates greed, making theft a new art form, and welfare fraud is condemned as proof that the poor can't be trusted. The warnings are posted on the economic beaches—a great depression may soon ensue.

Religious fanatics have now become convinced that the end of the world is in view. The year 2000 seems to them a logical time. They sound the knell; the death rattle for civilization is now in progress, they claim.

Many wonder why our Blessed Mother is appearing daily to the children in Yugoslavia. The scriptural message of prayer and penance sounds in a new wilderness, John the Baptist revisited. Fasting has revived an ancient tradition; a healthy spiritual heart instead of a hard body is the goal.

Our Blessed Mother promised a sign would be left; then the trials will begin. A short period of time will be left for repentance. "Conversions will abound," Mary said. Then the trials will take place, she has warned.

I believe Mary may have already left part of that sign—the cross itself, on the mountain. Many have seen the cross on Mount Kriesevac appear lighted by a neon like glow at night time. The cross has changed colors; red as the bloody waters of the red tide; gold as the promise of peace. I have seen a picture of myself in front of the cross; one copy turned red, the other yellow. The rosary beads appear under the cross. The testimony of the children in Slidell points to the cross as a possible sign.

The pilgrims to Medjugorje may also be part of that sign. They are a witness to the world of a new kind of miracle—conversion, healing of sinful memories, and peace of soul.

This small work is testimony of a sinful priest to the powerful conversion offered by Jesus Christ through His Mother, Mary. I am a witness given to every Catholic priest throughout the world that Mary loves every priest despite our problems. Our Blessed Mother lay to rest my damning perfectionism and flooded my heart with forgiveness and peace. I now know that Mary loves me. She loves each of you, and if Mary loves us, certainly Jesus does as well.

Peace is a journey; it is a gift from Jesus Christ. It begins with repentance and forgiveness of sins. Once inside our hearts, the Lord Jesus cures our self-hatred through a healing of memories, and peace of soul occurs.

Countless pilgrims to Medjugorje have seen little signs: a wounded sinful heart healed, troubled souls annointed, a community of believers on fire with the love of Jesus Christ. The sign may be as simple as a rosary changing color or seeing the sun appear like a host with dancing colors surrounding it. I believe the golden cross was a sign for me. Addictions will be cured only through the cross of Jesus Christ. Prayer and penance are the biblical medicine prescribed by our Heavenly Mother.

Signs will not prove that Mary is appearing at Medjugorje. To those who want to believe, no signs will be necessary; to those who do not, signs will simply be a source of consternation. Signs prove nothing.

The cross changes color from red to gold. The trials will end; a period of peace will occur. The Lady who chose to call herself "Queen of Peace" promised it. In your darkest hour look to the cross of Jesus Christ. It alone can save you. Remember always that Mary's role today is what it has always been: to lead you to Jesus. Jesus alone saves.

MESSAGES OF OUR BLESSED MOTHER

PEACE

"I have come to Medjugorje to bring the word of peace and I want the Holy Father to take it to all the world."

When asked her name, Mary replied, "Queen of Peace."

CONVERSION

"Tell all my sons and daughters, tell the world, and as soon as you can, that I wish for their conversion. I shall pray that God may not put you to the test. You do not know, you cannot know or imagine what God is about to send upon the world if you do not convert.'

PRAYER

"You have all forgotten that it is through prayer and fasting that wars are dispelled; and if they have already started, they will stop. Even natural laws can be suspended."

"What is most necessary is prayer. Ask for the Holy Spirit to come down on earth, and then all will become clear and the world will change."

FASTING

"Fasting practically does not exist. We must renew it. Peace, conversion, the healing of the sick . . . are not found without prayer and fasting."

MASS

"Mass is the most excellent form of prayer."

POSTSCRIPT

The purpose of this book was not to prove that the apparitions at Medjugorje are true. It is rather a simple story of a priest who found peace when he rediscovered the love of his Heavenly Mother, Mary, and the impact on our community.

The message of Mary clearly involves a warning, but it is much more. It is all about peace. Our Blessed Mother realizes that 800 million Catholics cannot all go to Yugoslavia, but we can all have the peace she promises. That peace is found in community.

The Holy Spirit taught us that two ingredients are required for peace, forgiveness and affirmation or love. We discovered this on a peer ministry retreat at Destin, Florida. There were seventeen teens and thirteen others, including children and adults.

The first two days of the retreat were filled with affirmation. I have never felt so loved, so embraced by our young people. It was marvelous. I will always treasure a gift from three of my girls, a key chain with the words "Dad's Keys."

We had arrived at Destin Friday afternoon. By Saturday night I was ecstatic. Then I learned that discord had set in; we were being torn apart by rumor and rancor. Whenever the Holy Spirit is active, Satan steps in to sow discord.

Then something amazing happened to the young people. Four of them, unable to sleep early Sunday morning, went walking on the beach. One of them looked up at the moon. Clouds began to peel away. Lori could not believe her eyes. It was the Blessed Mother. She turned to one of her friends.

"I know, Lori," April said. "She is beautiful."

The other two girls saw a blue color around the moon.

Within an hour we were all awakened. There was a strong aroma of roses just outside our condo. We made our way to the beach, and the group recited the Rosary. Our Lady had given us a little sign and like small children, we were overjoyed. We returned to bed at three in the morning.

Later in the day we discussed these events. Five of the teens had seen Mary. They described a sense of warmth, an incredible love of a mother. Some had seen the blue around the moon that I had witnessed. Some saw a perfect rainbow around it. Another saw a cross in the sky. Most had smelled the fragrance of roses. All had a sense of peace.

The discussion now turned to the problem that threatened to divide us. Angie rose and read a poem on friendship. She then gave the greatest talk on forgiveness I have ever heard. She concluded by saying, "We only have each other . . . we only have each other." Then she broke down and sobbed.

Everyone was moved to tears. I reminded the group that Our Blessed Mother told the Pastor at Medjugorje that failure to forgive blocks the power of the Holy Spirit. It was only when the entire congregation at St. James cried out, "I forgive," that their community of love was formed.

The adults left this condo and went to another to say the Rosary. The teens were told to ask each other for forgiveness. After we left, they broke down the chief barrier to community; they forgave one another. The Holy Spirit had formed another community through forgiveness and love.

A week later at the Sunday 7:00 P.M. Mass a number of teens shared their story at the homily. Grown men and women were deeply moved. In place of the sign of peace, we spent a few moments in silence asking forgiveness in our hearts. Some of us needed to forgive ourselves as well as others.

After communion I told the congregation that the Holy Spirit would pour out His Grace upon us since we had forgiven each other, but we needed to feel loved. The priest can make

Christ present on the altar at the Eucharist. Only you can make Him present in the pews by letting your sisters and brothers feel loved. We cannot feel loved by Christ if we do not believe we are loved by others or loved by ourselves.

Mike Clavijo, a Slidell High senior, then sang a song he had written titled "I Give My Heart to You." It is about a statue in a cathedral in Germany. During the war the arms were blown off and they wanted to destroy the statue. Instead, they put a plaque under it that said: "He has no hands but yours."

"Jesus wants to embrace each of us," I said, "but the only hands he has are yours. Would you spend a few moments sharing your love with one another?"

For fifteen minutes there was an incredible outpouring of love. Once again the Holy Spirit was forming a community of love through forgiveness and affirmation. It was Pentecost Sunday.

The following Saturday the peer ministry group assembled over one hundred teens for a youth rally. Once again these courageous young people shared Mary's love.

Each of them now wore a shirt with the theme of the day, "Embraced." A sketch on the shirt included five figures under a cross. One of the parents had seen the teens on their knees in prayer together on a walk near the beach. Michael had drawn the picture of a scene that deeply moved him.

The rally ended with Mass. I reminded the group about the story of the Old Abbot. Discouraged because his monastery was no longer attracting the young, he went walking in the woods. There he discovered a rabbi.

"Can you give me any encouragement?" he asked.

"Tell them the Messiah is among you," he said. "Tell them the Messiah is among you."

Upon his return, the abbot shared the message. The monks were incredulous. They knew the faults of one another.

But suppose, they thought, *it might be true*. Since they did not know which one was the Messiah, they treated each other with genuine love.

The word began to spread. People were touched by the love of that community. Young people flocked to join.

"Our parish community will become that enclave of love," I said, "if you truly embrace, truly love one another. We know from the Acts of the Apostles that the Church was spread by word of mouth—'See how they love one another.' "

The Holy Spirit is beginning to form a living, exciting community in Slidell. The peace promised by Our Lady is taking form.

You do not need to go to Medjugorje to get that peace. Prayer, penance, and fasting will prepare your soul to receive it.

But first, you need forgiveness. Many hold onto anger, resentment, and hatred. Nothing blocks the power of the Spirit like the inability to forgive. I believe this is why Mary encourages Catholics to go to confession once a month. Forgiveness is the key to peace.

Once you have forgiven yourself and others, you are then ready for the Holy Spirit to form you into a true community. The final step is love or affirmation.

There is an incredible hunger for the love of Jesus Christ in the world. Eighty million Americans alone are unchurched. But they will never experience the love of Jesus until they feel your love. The moment they are embraced by you, the love of Christ becomes real. Jesus has no hands . . . but yours.

I believe the trials predicted by Our Blessed Mother may well be here already. Addictions are now epidemic. Only the Cross of Jesus Christ can cure them.

There will be enclaves, communities where the Holy Spirit is alive. It is my fervent hope that every Catholic parish become that harbor of peace by living the messages of Our Lady.

Buffeted by the power of Satan, seek the shelter envisioned by Our Lady at Medjurgorje.

This small work was meant primarily for my fellow priests, to share with them what they already know, that Mary loves priests with an incredible love. In Mary's eyes you are cherished. You are her sons.

But I wrote this book for the laymen as well. You do not need to go to Medjugorje to live the messages of Our Lady—prayer, penance, the Rosary, the Mass, and monthly confession. It is not necessary to see signs in order to feel the love of our Mother. Signs do not prove anything—love does. Live the messages and peace will be yours.

Finally, I believe the Holy Spirit will make your parish a warm, vibrant, loving community through forgiveness and affirmation. This will result in an incredible peace.

Once again Our Blessed Mother is doing what she does best, bringing us to Jesus Christ. Never forget the promise of Christ. "Peace is my gift to you!"